Religious Topics

RELIGIOUS SERVICES

Jon Mayled

Religious Topics

Art and Architecture
Birth Customs
Death Customs
Family Life
Feasting and Fasting
Holy Books

Initiation Rites
Marriage Customs
Pilgrimage
Religious Dress
Religious Services
Teachers and Prophets

Cover *Taking the* Torah *scrolls from the Ark.*

First published in 1986 by Wayland (Publishers) Limited
61 Western Road, Hove, East Sussex BN3 1JD, England

© Copyright 1986 Wayland (Publishers) Limited

British Library Catalouguing in Publication Data
Mayled, Jon
    Religious services. – (Religious topics)
    1. Public worship – Juvenile literature
    I. Title II. Series
    291.3 BL550

ISBN 0–85078–771–8

Phototypeset by Kalligraphics Ltd., Redhill, Surrey
Printed in Italy by G. Canale & C.S.p.A., Turin
Bound in Belgium by Casterman S.A.

Contents

Introduction

All the religions of the world have some kind of organized worship. In this book we shall look at the very different ways in which people worship. During these services people have an opportunity to feel very close to their god. They worship their god and may give thanks for what has happened to them or ask for help in their lives or for other people.

Prayer is a very important part of all religious services. Worshippers believe that it gives them the chance to speak directly to their god.

Some religious services are very quiet and formal events. During others, worshippers may sing and play music to show how happy they are at the chance to worship their god.

Although people may hold special services to celebrate religious festivals, most faiths have daily or weekly acts of worship as well.

Some Christian religious services are very formal events.

Muslims gather together to pray outside a mosque.

Some services are congregational, which means that everyone gathers together to worship. On other occasions people may worship on their own or with their family at home.

Buddhism

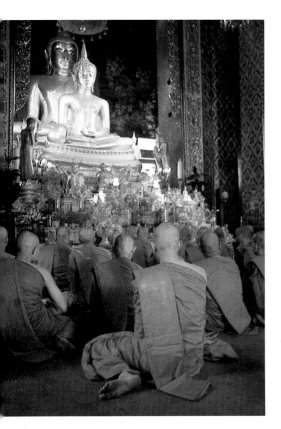

During the service Buddhist monks pray to the Buddha.

There are two different groups of Buddhists and they worship in different ways.

Theravada Buddhists come from India, Sri Lanka, Burma and Thailand. Although Buddhists may gather together in one temple to worship, they each say their own personal prayers.

Many temples are filled with flowers and paper lamps and incense is burned. Outside there may be stalls selling paper umbrellas, flowers, incense sticks and statues, which the worshippers can buy as gifts. When people enter the temples they bow, then kneel and then lie on the ground. They pray to the Buddha and offer their gifts to the Three Jewels, which are the Buddha, the *Dharma* (the teachings), and the *sangha* (the monks). They ring bells as they offer their gifts.

The *Mahayana* Buddhists of China and

The Wheel of Life has six sections which portray the different states of mind that people go through.

Tibet worship in buildings shaped like pagodas. These are built in special places and have several halls inside. In each hall there are statues with tables in front for incense and flowers.

Each prayer wheel has a prayer inscribed on to it.

Many people go to the temple to seek answers to questions about the future. They throw two semi-circular pieces of red wood on to the ground. Depending on which way these fall the worshippers take a piece of paper or wood from a particular drawer. They hand this to the priest who then selects the appropriate answer from a list. This answer, they believe, tells them something about what will happen to them. Sometimes they spin the Wheel of Life and take their answer according to which section it stops at. The Wheel of Life has six sections which portray the different states of mind people go through.

Like *Theravada* Buddhists, *Mahayana* Buddhists worship individually. Buddhists in Tibet can please the gods by walking around the temple and reciting Buddhist texts. Sometimes they carry prayer wheels, which can also be found inside the temple. A prayer wheel is a cylinder which has a prayer inscribed on it. The movement sets up a vibration which carries the prayer in every direction to all parts of the world.

Buddhist monks pray in the temples every day, while the worshippers light incense and turn the many prayer wheels.

Every Mahayana *temple has a set of prayer wheels.*

9

Chinese

In China, many people follow the Taoist religion. Their temples are called *kuans* and are looked after by monks.

Worshippers go to the *kuan* to offer prayers and to burn incense to the gods. People bow to the altar while holding sticks of burning incense in their hands.

Taoists sometimes go to the *kuan* to ask the priests questions about what they should do for the future. People also go to the *kuan* on the birthday of a god. The god's statue is carried on a carriage, called a *palanquin*, surrounded by gongs and firecrackers.

Taoist monks place great importance on peace and tranquillity.

Christianity

Christians who belong to different denominations or groups, worship in different ways. However, the most common service in the Christian Church is one where the worshippers eat and drink bread and wine together. This is called by several names: the Mass, the Eucharist, Holy Communion and the Lord's Supper. Usually this service takes place in a church, though it can be celebrated anywhere.

Mass being celebrated in Vellore, southern India.

Communion plays an important part in the Christian religious service. It commemorates the Last Supper which Jesus ate with his disciples. This service is taking place in Bethlehem.

At this service Christians remember how, on the night before he died, Jesus ate the Last Supper with his disciples. At this meal he shared bread and wine with them and said:

'Take, eat; this is my body which is given for you: do this in remembrance of me.

Drink ye all of this; for this is my blood of the New Testament which is shed for you and for many for the remission of sins: do this as oft as ye shall drink it, in remembrance of me.'

In the Roman Catholic Church the Eucharist begins by the people telling God that they have sinned and asking him to forgive them. This is followed by two readings from the Bible, usually one from the Old Testament and one from the New.

Then people all say the Creed together. This is a prayer which states what Christians believe about God and Jesus. People then pray to God for the Church and for the troubles of the world.

The work of the Church costs money and after the sermon a collection of money is made

People prepare to take Communion from a Roman Catholic priest in Brazil.

Baptists have quite informal services characterized by music and hymn singing. This service is taking place in Indianapolis, USA.

from the congregation. Next, bread, in the form of small wafers, and wine is taken up to the altar. The priest blesses these and repeats the words of Jesus at the Last Supper. There then follows a communal saying of the 'Our Father' prayer and the priest and congregation wish each other peace in God's name. Then the wafers are distributed to the worshippers.

Sometimes this service takes place with many ceremonies, music and singing of hymns but on other occasions it can be very short and simple.

Hinduism

Although Hindus may worship in a temple (*mandir*), their most important holy place is the home. Homes have a room or a corner set apart for worship. There are pictures or statues of the family's favourite gods or goddesses.

Puja (worship) is the responsibility of the woman in the household. In the morning, after having a shower, she prays and then washes and dresses the statue or offers

Hindu homes have a room or corner set apart for worship. For Hindus, the home is the most important holy place.

Hindus decorate the statues of their god, Brahman, with flowers, as part of their religious services.

flowers, incense, light (*diva*) and food (*parshad*) to the gods. This *parshad* is added to the food which the family will eat.

In the evening the *diva* is lit before any other lights and members of the family join together to pray.

At dawn in the *mandir* the priest washes and dresses the statue of the god. They usually have a different set of clothes for every day of the year. Flowers and food are offered and incense is burned while the priest chants the *Vedas* which is a Hindu holy scripture. Later, worshippers come to light candles and say prayers.

As they leave the temple they are given *parshad*. In the evening the priest performs ceremonies to put the gods to bed.

When people are gathered together in the temple to worship, the service is made up of three parts: the kindling of the fire; worship of the eight and singing of the *bhajans*. Firstly the priest lights the sacred fire of wood, camphor and ghee, and sections from the *Vedas* are chanted. Then the *arti* tray is moved slowly in front of the gods.

Next a spot of *kum-kum* (red paste) is placed on the foreheads of the statues, of the

A Hindu priest chants the Vedas *in the* mandir *during a religious service in Nepal.*

17

In the arti *ceremony an oil lamp is held before the statue of a god and moved in front of it in a circular pattern to form a circle of light.*

pictures and of the worshippers. Then the *arti* tray is carried around to all the people in the temple. They hold their hands over the top of the flames and then pass their hands over their foreheads and hair.

Finally, *parshad* is distributed to the worshippers and hymns (*bhajans*) are sung. Sometimes people dance which is also a form of worship.

During the course of the service there may also be readings from the Hindu scriptures and a talk.

Islam

All Muslims must worship God, *Allah*, five times a day in prayer. Before praying people must wash their hands; their mouth and nose,

Mecca is the religious centre of Islam.

then their face; their right hand and arm then their left; their head and finally their ears and feet. This is in the *Qur'an*. It is to ensure that the worshippers are clean and pure for prayer. As the water is cold water it makes the worshippers alert and able to concentrate on what they are about to do. After this the worshippers, wherever they are in the world, face in the direction of the *Kabba* in Mecca. The *Kabba* is a shrine in the city of Mecca, the religious centre of Islam, which contains a holy Black Stone.

These prayers (*salat*) take place at daybreak (*fajr*), at midday (*zuhr*), in the afternoon (*'asr*), in the evening (*maghrib*) and at night (*'isha*). Muslims must try to carry out their prayers as near to these times as possible. Muslims pray in different positions: standing, kneeling and touching the ground with their foreheads. A prayer mat is necessary to ensure that the place of prayer is clean and to keep the body clean during prayer.

A Muslim in Chad, north Africa, prays on his prayer mat.

20

The Muslim place of worship is called a mosque. In Muslim countries these buildings are often large, square buildings with a dome. Outside is a courtyard with water for washing before prayer. There will be at least one tall tower called a minaret. It is from here that a person called the *muezzin* calls people to pray five times a day.

The muezzin *calls people to prayer from a tall tower called a minaret.*

Prayers may be offered in any clean place, even in the street. These Muslims in Cairo have removed their shoes as a sign of respect to Allah.

All Muslim men are expected to go to the mosque for the midday prayer on Fridays. Women can also go but they sit separately from the men. Everyone must remove their shoes when they enter the mosque.

In the mosque is a pulpit called a *minbar*. It is here that the leader of the local community, the *Imam*, stands when he is giving the Friday sermon, the *khutba*. This sermon is in two parts. The first usually deals with particular problems of everyday life and the second discusses a particular passage from the *Qur'an*.

Judaism

The Jewish Sabbath begins on Friday night and lasts until Saturday evening. According to the *Tenakh*, the Jewish holy scriptures, it was on this day that God rested after he had created the world. The Ten Commandments say:

'Observe the Sabbath day, to keep it holy.'

Orthodox, or strict, Jews do not do any work on the Sabbath. Although there is a service at the synagogue on Friday evening, the main act of worship takes place on Saturday. Both men and women attend the synagogue. In an orthodox synagogue men and women sit separately but non-orthodox Jews sit together.

The service is in Hebrew and the singing is not accompanied by music. There are readings from the Psalms and then the Cantor sings the *Shema*. The Cantor is a man trained

Worshippers in the oldest synagogue in north Africa, at Djerba, Tunisia.

23

to sing sections of the service.

Next the people turn towards the Ark. This is a curtained cupboard which contains the *Torah* scrolls. On these scrolls are written the first five books of the *Tenakh*. The readings from the *Torah* scrolls are all in Hebrew.

The scrolls are covered with beautiful cloths and the cases have silver bells and ornaments on them. These indicate the

Taking the scrolls of the Torah *from the Ark.*

special place it has in the minds and lives of the people and the sweet tinkling of the bells as it is carried to the reading desk, indicate the sweetness and joy that the message of the reading has for the congregation. As the scrolls are lifted out of the Ark this prayer is said.

> *'This is the Law of Moses set before the Children of Israel . . .'*

The men touch the scrolls with their *Tallith* (a prayer shawl) and members of the congregation read from the scriputres.

After the readings the scrolls are returned to the Ark and the rabbi may give a sermon. Finally the *Kaddish* is said and the congregation reply:

> *'Let His name be blessed for ever and for all Eternity.'*

Jews also celebrate the Sabbath at home with a special family meal.

A rabbi delivers his sermon during a Sabbath service in Gibraltar.

Shintoism

In Japan, Shinto temples are called *jinjas*. Every day the priests renew the branches of the holy *sakaki* tree and clap their hands to wake the gods, *kami*. When there are worshippers in the *jinja* the priests perform songs and dances about the gods.

The *jinja* does not hold any religious services where people can worship together. People go to the *jinja* and ring bells to tell the gods they have arrived, then offer gifts and bow in prayer.

The followers of Shinto also go the *jinja* to find help and guidance for the future.

A jinja *(temple) in Tokyo, Japan.*

Sikhism

Sikhs worship in a temple called a *gurdwara*. They do not worship on a special day of the week, but always on a day suitable to the whole community.

In the centre of the *gurdwara* is a *takht* (throne) covered with a canopy. On the *takht* is placed the *Guru Granth Sahib*, the Sikh holy book.

When they enter the *gurdwara* people remove their shoes. They give money, food or a romalla (a cloth to cover the *Guru Granth Sahib*) and place them in front of the *takht*.

Above *A Sikh* gurdwara.

Sikh worshippers in a gurdwara *in Birmingham.*

27

During Sikh services people sometimes dance to the accompaniment of sitars and drums.

Men wear turbans in the *gurdwara* and the women cover their heads with a *dupatta* (a silk scarf). Shoes are not worn as a sign of respect.

The worshippers (*sangat*) sit cross-legged on the floor. Men and women must sit separately. There are readings from the *Guru Granth Sahib* by the leader of the worship, called the *Granthi*. The people sing hymns (*kirtan*) accompanied by sitars and drums. After this there will be a sermon and more singing, readings and prayers. The language of worship is Punjabi which is the language of the scriptures and of most Sikhs.

At the end of the service, which may last up to five hours, everyone shares *karah parshad*. This is a mixture of flour, semolina, ghee and sugar, eaten by everyone in order to show that they are all equal and that no one goes away hungry from the presence of God. Finally they go to the Guru's kitchen, called the *langar*, and eat a free meal together.

Women prepare food in the langar *for the meal eaten by everyone after the service.*

Glossary

Buddha Meaning the 'Awakened One'. The Buddha was Siddhartha Gautama, the son of an Indian King who lived about 4,500 years ago. Gautama gave up all his wealth in order to dedicate himself to following a religious life.

Dharma The teachings of the Buddha.

Disciples The twelve men who followed Jesus during his earthly life.

Eucharist A religious ceremony of the Lord's Supper, often called Holy Communion or the Mass.

Granthi A leader of Sikh worship who looks after the *Guru Granth Sahib*.

Gurdwara A Sikh place of worship. The word means 'House of God'.

Guru Granth Sahib The Sikh Holy Book, which contains 5,894 hymns and verses.

Imam A prayer-leader in a mosque.

Kuan Taoist place of worship.

Langar The name for the kitchen and the food which is prepared and eaten at the *gurdwara* after a service. It symbolizes unity and equality amongst Sikhs.

Minbar The pulpit in a mosque.

Mosque The Muslim place of worship.

Parshad A holy food.

Rabbi Leader of a Jewish community.

Romalla The cloth used to cover the *Guru Granth Sahib*.

Further Reading

Salat A Muslim prayer.

Sangha The community of Buddhist monks and nuns.

Shema The first prayer learned by Jewish children, and last spoken by the dying.

Synagogue The Jewish place of worship and meeting.

If you would like to find out more about religious services, you may like to read the following books:

Beliefs and Believers series – published by Wayland

Exploring Religion series – published by Bell and Hyman

Religions of the World series – published by Wayland

Worship series – published by Holt Saunders

The following videos are very helpful:

Islam – produced by ILEA Learning Resources.

The Jesus Project – produced by CEM Video, 2 Chester House, Pages Lane, London N10.

Through the Eyes series – produced by CEM Video.

Acknowledgements

The publisher would like to thank the following for providing the pictures for this book: Bruce Coleman 7; Jimmy Holmes 9; Hutchison Library 13, 14, 15, 20, 21, 26, 27 (top); Anne and Bury Peerless 11, 18; M.P. Walters 27 (bottom); Zefa *cover*, 4, 5, 6, 8, 10, 12, 16, 17, 19, 22, 23, 24, 25.

Index